We Have a Constitution

Ann Bonwill

Content Consultant

Kerry Sautner, Chief Learning Officer
National Constitution Center, Philadelphia, Pennsylvania

Reading Consultant

Jeanne M. Clidas, Ph.D.
Reading Specialist

Children's Press®
An Imprint of Scholastic Inc.

Library of Congress Cataloging-in-Publication Data
Names: Bonwill, Ann, author.
Title: We have a constitution/By Ann Bonwill.
Description: New York: Children's Press, an Imprint of Scholastic Inc., 2019. |
Series: Rookie read-about civics | Includes bibliographical references and index.
Identifiers: LCCN 2018032592 | ISBN 9780531129159 (library binding: alk. paper) |
ISBN 9780531137734 (pbk.: alk. paper)
Subjects: LCSH: Constitutional law—United States—Juvenile literature.
Classification: LCC KF4550.Z9 B66 2019 | DDC 342.7302—dc23

Produced by Spooky Cheetah Press
Design: Keith Plechaty/kwpCreative
Creative Direction: Judith E. Christ for Scholastic Inc.

Published in 2019 by Children's Press, an imprint of Scholastic Inc.

Printed in North Mankato, MN, USA   113

1 2 3 4 5 6 7 8 9 10 R 28 27 26 25 24 23 22 21 20 19

Scholastic, Inc., 557 Broadway, New York, NY 10012.

Photographs © cover: Ariel Skelley/Getty Images; cover background: Steve McAlister/Getty Images; cover flag bunting: LiveStock/Shutterstock; 3 bottom center: Susan Law Cain/Shutterstock; 3 bottom right: Sibrikov Valery/Shutterstock; 4: Ken Karp Photography; 7: D. Hurst/Alamy Images; 8: CCI/Bridgeman Images; 11: Bettmann/Getty Images; 13: Sean Pavone/Shutterstock; 14: Tetra Images/Getty Images; 17 buildings: JPL Designs/Shutterstock; 17 tree: Shendart/iStockphoto; 19 top: PhotosIndia.com LLC/Alamy Images; 19 bottom: Thierry Gouegnon/Reuters; 20: Bettmann/Getty Images; 23: Yellow Dog Productions/Getty Images; 25: Bettmann/Getty Images; 27: Michael Ventura/Alamy Images; 28: John Melton Collection, Oklahoma Historical Society Research Division; 29: Courtesy of Ayanna Najuma; 30 center: saiva/iStockphoto; 30 bottom right: Sibrikov Valery/Shutterstock; 31 top right: Jim McMahon/Mapman ®; 31 center right, convention: Bettmann/Getty Images; 31 center right, Constitution: D. Hurst/Alamy Images; 31 bottom right: CCI/Bridgeman Images.

Table of Contents

I have my

☑ coat
☑ backpack
☑ book
☑ homework sheet

CHAPTER 1

What Is the Constitution?

Rules are everywhere! At home we are expected to pick up our toys, wash our hands before dinner, and tell our parents the truth. At school we are asked to line up quietly, do our homework, and share with our classmates.

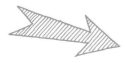 What is one of the rules in your classroom?

Our country has rules, too. They are called laws. Our country's major laws are written in a **document** called the Constitution. These laws describe the powers of our government. They also describe the rights and responsibilities of citizens of the United States.

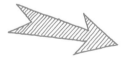 What are some of your responsibilities at home?

We the People of the United States, in order to form a more perfect Union, establish Justice, insure domestic Tranquility, provide for the common defence, promote the general Welfare, and secure the Blessings of Liberty to ourselves and our Posterity, do ordain and establish this Constitution for the United States of America.

Article. I.

Section. 1. ...

Section. 2. ...

Section. 3. The Senate of the United States ...

Section. 4. The Times, Places and Manner of holding Elections for Senators and Representatives, shall be prescribed in each State by the Legislature thereof ...

Section. 5. Each House shall be the Judge of the Elections, Returns and Qualifications of its own Members ...

Section. 6. The Senators and Representatives shall receive a Compensation for their Services, to be ascertained by Law, and paid out of the Treasury of the United States ...

Section. 7. All Bills for raising Revenue shall originate in the House of Representatives; but the Senate may propose or concur with Amendments as on other Bills.

Every Bill which shall have passed the House of Representatives and the Senate, shall, before it become a Law, be presented to the President of the ...

American colonists dumped British tea into the sea to show their disapproval of British taxes.

CHAPTER 2

Early Days

Native Americans were the first people in North America. Then settlers from Europe began to arrive. By 1752, there were 13 English **colonies** here. Leaders across the sea made laws for the colonies. Colonists had to pay **taxes**. That money was used to make things better in England—not in America. Many colonists thought this was unfair.

The American Revolutionary War lasted from 1775 to 1783. The colonists won their freedom. The United States of America had become a country!

After the war, the 13 new states had trouble working together. In 1787, a group of leaders gathered in Philadelphia, Pennsylvania, to figure out how our country should be run. They wrote down our new laws in the Constitution.

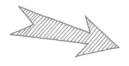 When do we celebrate America's birthday?

Many leaders helped write the Constitution, including James Madison, Alexander Hamilton, Benjamin Franklin, and George Washington. These leaders did not always agree. They held meetings to decide which laws were the most important. They had to **compromise**.

 How do you compromise with your friends?

The Constitution was signed in this building in Philadelphia, Pennsylvania.

CHAPTER 3

Laws of the Land

The Constitution allows us to choose our leaders. People vote for their leaders. Every four years, we vote for our country's president. The president makes a promise to follow and protect our Constitution.

 Who was our country's first president?

The Constitution sets up three branches of government. It divides the power among the different branches. No one branch has too much control over the others. The branches have to work together in order to make changes and get things done.

 Why is it important to share power?

The Three Branches of Government

The **legislative branch** is in charge of making laws. The Senate and the House of Representatives make up this branch.

The **executive branch** is in charge of making sure laws are obeyed. The president is the head of the executive branch.

The **judicial branch** is in charge of deciding the meaning of laws and whether they break the rules of the Constitution.

The Constitution sets out the rights and freedoms of citizens of the United States. One important freedom is that people are allowed to practice any religion they would like. Muslims can celebrate Ramadan. Christians can celebrate Christmas. Hindus can celebrate Diwali. People can practice other religions, too—or none at all.

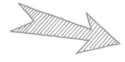 What does it mean to be free?

Diwali

Ramadan

Leaders worked on the Constitution from May to September 1787.

CHAPTER 4

Open to Change

The Constitution was written more than 200 years ago. But it is not the same today as it was then. The Constitution has changed and grown. It now has 27 amendments. Amendments are changes that have been made to the Constitution.

 Why would people want to change the Constitution?

The first 10 amendments to the Constitution are called the Bill of Rights. This section of the Constitution was added in 1791. It promises people certain freedoms, such as the right to speak freely.

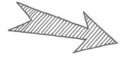 Is it OK to say what you believe?

INDIAN
OCEAN
AUSTRALIA
15 30 45 60 75 90 105 120 135 150 165 180 East Longitude
Vertical Exaggeration 100 to 1
12 13 14 15 16 17 18 19 20
22 23 24 25 26 27 28 29 30
32 33 34 35 36 37 38 39 40
52 53 54 55 56 57 58 59 60
63 64 65 66 67 68 69 70
73 74 75 76 77 78 79 80
83 84 85 86 87 88 89 90
94 95 96 97 98 99 100
105 106 107 108 109 110

Over the years, more changes have been made to the Constitution. The 13th Amendment was added in 1865. It made slavery illegal. In 1920, the 19th Amendment gave women the right to vote.

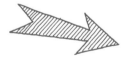 **What would you add to the Constitution?**

The original Constitution is on display in Washington, D.C. More than one million people have visited it.

We celebrate Constitution Day every year on September 17. It is a day to remember that the Constitution is still important for our country. It belongs to us all!

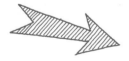 Why is it important to have a constitution?

A family visits the original Constitution at the National Archives in Washington, D.C.

Kids Can Make

In 1958, Ayanna was seven years old. In her town, African Americans like her were not allowed to use the same water fountains as white people. They could not go to the same schools or eat at the same restaurants.

Ayanna and her friends did not think this was fair. They wanted to do something about it.

Ayanna in 1958

a Difference!

Ayanna and her friends went to a restaurant that served only white people. They sat at the counter and tried to order food, but no one would serve them. They had to go back three days in a row, but finally they were given their food.

Ayanna and her friends, and others like them, stood up for

Ayanna today

what they believed. Their right to speak up is protected by the Constitution. Their brave actions led to the creation of new laws. These laws protect the freedoms of all people, no matter the color of their skin.

29

Our country's major laws are written in a document called the Constitution. It is important to remember some key facts about it. Which can you remember?

☑ The Constitution was written in 1787.

☑ The Constitution was signed in Philadelphia.

☑ The Constitution describes the powers of the government.

☑ The Constitution sets out our rights and freedoms.

☑ The Bill of Rights was added to the Constitution in 1791.

☑ The 13th Amendment outlawed slavery in 1865.

☑ The 19th Amendment gave women the right to vote in 1920.

☑ The Constitution is on display in Washington, D.C.

Glossary

colonies (**kah**-luh-neez): territories settled and controlled by people from another country
▶ *The American* **colonies** *fought for independence.*

compromise (**kahm**-pruh-mize): to accept just some of what you want to satisfy some requests of others
▶ *Leaders had to* **compromise** *when drafting the Constitution.*

document (**dahk**-yuh-muhnt): paper containing official information
▶ *The Constitution is a very important* **document**.

taxes (**taks**-ez): money people pay in order to support a government
▶ *American colonists did not want to pay* **taxes** *to the British.*

Index

Facts for Now

Visit this Scholastic website to learn more about the U.S. Constitution:

www.factsfornow.scholastic.com

Enter the keyword **Constitution**

About the Author

Ann Bonwill enjoys writing books for children. She lives near Washington, D.C., and has visited the original Constitution with her family.